Cloze
in on Language

Ages 5-7

Ancient People

Under the Sea

Transport

Discovering the Past

Seasons

Harsh Environments

Disasters

Endangered Animals

Literature

Women of Courage

Environment

Legendary Heroes

Special Days

Communication

Health

Great Inventions

Famous Voyages

by George Moore
World Teachers Press

Published with the permission of R.I.C. Publications Pty. Ltd.

First published by R.I.C. Publications Pty. Ltd., Perth, Western Australia.

Printed in the United States of America.

Order Number 2-5055
ISBN 1-885111-69-X

   D E F   01

Educational Resources

395 Main Street
Rowley, MA 01969

This series of four books is a challenging language package, based on a cloze format, covering an approximate age range from 7 - 12 years. Each topic contains cloze text followed by comprehension activities based on the three levels of questioning and activity pages which follow modern educational trends.

The cloze text contains a mixture of fiction and nonfiction information, with some topics reflecting the interest in schools and the wider community over subjects such as: endangered animals, ancient civilizations, pollution, courageous women, transportation, inventions, health issues and literature.

Two teacher information pages are included to demonstrate how to get the most benefit from each book and answers have been provided to save you valuable preparation time.

About the Author

George Moore has been a practicing classroom teacher for over 30 years, with experience in primary and secondary areas. He has held promotional positions in England, New South Wales and Western Australia.

Contents

Cloze in on Language has been written to develop reading skills through cloze procedures. This approach has been well-tried and proven. *Cloze in on Language* adds further dimensions by including detailed comprehension activities and a variety of language activities which include:

- Word study
- Time lines
- Read and draw
- Retrieval charts
- Labeling
- Grids

Cloze

It is suggested that the *Cloze* sheet for each topic is completed first and corrected before the *Comprehension* sheets and *Activities* are attempted. This means that a complete and correct text is available for study in order to answer the *Comprehension* questions and to complete the *Activities*.

The topics themselves are of perennial interest to students. They draw on subjects from literature and history and touch on concerns of importance to us all today, such as pollution and endangered animals.

Discuss the topic of the cloze activity as a class or group discussion. Draw on existing knowledge and experience which can be shared with other class members

Explain how words can be located by reading the words around the space and then matching against the words at the bottom of the page.

Note: When answering, discuss other suitable words that could be used to make sense of the text. This is important to show that there is not always only one correct answer.

For advanced readers an alternative is to complete the activity without access to the words at the bottom of the page.

Comprehension

The *Comprehension* activities contain a balance of:

- literal
- inferential
- evaluative questions

These question types encourage the use of reading skills such as cause and effect, main ideas and context clues. Comprehension activities can be completed in written form as well as class and group discussion. Discussion is an important part of this process, especially with inferential and evaluative questions where there may not be only one correct answer or opinion.

Literal *Comprehension* questions. This encourages students to read and comprehend accurately. In most cases there will be only one correct answer.

Inferential *Comprehension* questions. This encourages students to infer the answer from surrounding text and existing knowledge. Students should be encouraged to justify their answers with supporting facts.

Evaluative *Comprehension* questions. This encourages students to provide opinions and thoughts on the subject matter without needing to be right or wrong.

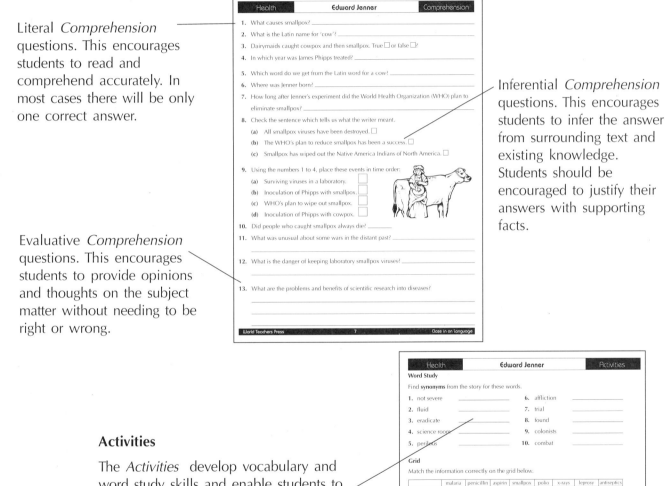

| Health | Edward Jenner | Comprehension |

1. What causes smallpox? _____
2. What is the Latin name for 'cow'? _____
3. Dairymaids caught cowpox and then smallpox. True ☐ or false ☐?
4. In which year was James Phipps treated? _____
5. Which word do we get from the Latin word for a cow? _____
6. Where was Jenner born? _____
7. How long after Jenner's experiment did the World Health Organization (WHO) plan to eliminate smallpox? _____
8. Check the sentence which tells us what the writer meant.
   (a) All smallpox viruses have been destroyed. ☐
   (b) The WHO's plan to reduce smallpox has been a success. ☐
   (c) Smallpox has wiped out the Native America Indians of North America. ☐
9. Using the numbers 1 to 4, place these events in time order:
   (a) Surviving viruses in a laboratory. ☐
   (b) Inoculation of Phipps with smallpox. ☐
   (c) WHO's plan to wipe out smallpox. ☐
   (d) Inoculation of Phipps with cowpox. ☐
10. Did people who caught smallpox always die? _____
11. What was unusual about some wars in the distant past? _____
12. What is the danger of keeping laboratory smallpox viruses? _____
13. What are the problems and benefits of scientific research into diseases? _____

World Teachers Press   7   Cloze in on Language

Activities

The *Activities* develop vocabulary and word study skills and enable students to use research skills to seek further background information on the worksheet topics. They also give students the opportunity to use their imagination in exercises which delve into more creative aspects of the topics studied.

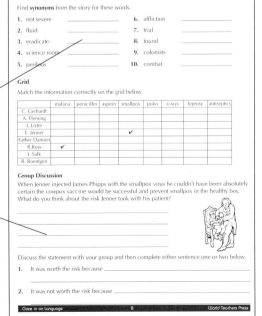

| Health | Edward Jenner | Activities |

Word Study

Find **synonyms** from the story for these words.

1. not severe _____   6. affliction _____
2. fluid _____   7. trial _____
3. eradicate _____   8. found _____
4. science room _____   9. colonists _____
5. perilous _____   10. combat _____

Grid

Match the information correctly on the grid below.

	malaria	penicillin	aspirin	smallpox	polio	x-rays	leprosy	antiseptics
C. Gerhardt								
A. Fleming								
J. Lister								
E. Jenner				✔				
Father Damien								
R. Ross	✔							
J. Salk								
R. Roentgen								

Group Discussion

When Jenner injected James Phipps with the smallpox virus he couldn't have been absolutely certain the cowpox vaccine would be successful and prevent smallpox in the healthy boy. What do you think about the risk Jenner took with his patient?

_____

_____

Discuss the statement with your group and then complete either sentence one or two below.

1. It was worth the risk because _____

2. It was not worth the risk because _____

Cloze in on Language   8   World Teachers Press

Smallpox is a disease that once killed millions. It is caused _____(1) spread from person to person through droplets _____(2) when someone coughs or sneezes. Many survivors were blinded or scarred _____(3).

The disease was so common _____ (4) that almost everyone caught it at some time.

_____(5) more soldiers died from smallpox than from fighting, and when European settlers carried the disease _____(6), millions of Native American Indians died.

In the 18th century healthy people were inoculated _____(7) from smallpox sores but it was dangerous as they could develop a serious kind of smallpox.

_____(8), Edward Jenner, discovered vaccination (from the Latin 'vacca', meaning 'a cow') as a way of protecting people _____(9). He realized that dairymaids who caught cowpox, _____ _____(10), did not catch smallpox. In 1796 he inoculated James Phipps, a boy aged eight, with pus _____(11) and James caught cowpox. Six weeks later Jenner inoculated him again with smallpox virus and it had no effect _____(12). His experiment was a success!

_____(13) the World Health Organization set out to eliminate smallpox altogether. A few years ago the only smallpox viruses left were _____(14).

to North America	for life	with liquid	In 1967
A British doctor	on the boy	from smallpox	in the air
by a virus	a mild cattle disease	in a laboratory	centuries ago
In some wars	from a dairymaid's sore		

1. What causes smallpox? _____

2. What is the Latin name for 'cow'? _____

3. Dairymaids caught cowpox and then smallpox. True ☐ or false ☐?

4. In which year was James Phipps treated? _____

5. Which word do we get from the Latin word for a cow? _____

6. Where was Jenner born? _____

7. How long after Jenner's experiment did the World Health Organization (WHO) plan to

   eliminate smallpox? _____

8. Check the sentence which tells us what the writer meant.

   (a) All smallpox viruses have been destroyed. ☐

   (b) The WHO's plan to reduce smallpox has been a success. ☐

   (c) Smallpox has wiped out the Native America Indians of North America. ☐

9. Using the numbers 1 to 4, place these events in time order:

   (a) Surviving viruses in a laboratory. ☐

   (b) Inoculation of Phipps with smallpox. ☐

   (c) WHO's plan to wipe out smallpox. ☐

   (d) Inoculation of Phipps with cowpox. ☐

10. Did people who caught smallpox always die? _____

11. What was unusual about some wars in the distant past? _____

    _____

12. What is the danger of keeping laboratory smallpox viruses? _____

    _____

13. What are the problems and benefits of scientific research into diseases?

    _____

    _____

    _____

Word Study

Find **synonyms** from the story for these words.

1. not severe _____
2. fluid _____
3. eradicate _____
4. science room _____
5. perilous _____

6. affliction _____
7. trial _____
8. found _____
9. colonists _____
10. combat _____

Grid

Match the information correctly on the grid below.

	malaria	penicillin	aspirin	smallpox	polio	x-rays	leprosy	antiseptics
C. Gerhardt								
A. Fleming								
J. Lister								
E. Jenner				✔				
Father Damien								
R.Ross	✔							
J. Salk								
R. Roentgen								

Group Discussion

When Jenner injected James Phipps with the smallpox virus he couldn't have been absolutely certain the cowpox vaccine would be successful and prevent smallpox in the healthy boy. What do you think about the risk Jenner took with his patient?

_____

_____

_____

_____

Discuss the statement with your group and then complete either sentence one or two below.

1. It was worth the risk because _____

_____

2. It was not worth the risk because _____

Hercules is the _____(1) name for the Greek legendary hero Herakles. Myths tell us he was courageous and _____(2). Hera, the wife of Zeus, King of the ancient gods, _____(3) Hercules, as Zeus had fathered him with another woman. She placed two venomous snakes into his _____(4) but the baby strangled them.

As a _____(5) man he was taught archery, wrestling and _____(6) by different experts. Later, in a fit of _____(7) caused by Hera, he killed his wife and children. As a punishment, for twelve years Hercules had to _____(8) the Greek king who made him perform the 'Twelve Labors of Hercules'.

These tasks included the slaying of the multi-headed _____(9) but as he cut off one head two grew in its place. Finally he slew the monster and used its blood to poison his _____(10). For his twelfth task Hercules _____(11) into the world of the dead to capture Cerberus, the three-headed watchdog _____(12) the underworld. Hercules also sailed with Jason in his _____(13) for the Golden Fleece.

When he died, Hercules was _____(14) to Mount Olympus, home of the gods, and became a god. He married a _____(15) of Hera, who had caused him so much trouble throughout his life.

arrows	cradle	guarding	daughter	serve
Roman	madness	Hydra	strong	search
descended	music	young	carried	hated

1. What terrible thing did Hercules do? _____

2. How long was Hercules punished for his crime? _____

3. What kind of animal guarded the world of the dead? _____

4. What does the word 'slew' mean? _____

5. Check the statement which tells us the main idea of paragraph three.

   (a) How Hercules became a god. ☐

   (b) The adventures of Hercules. ☐

   (c) The search for the Golden Fleece. ☐

6. Who was responsible for Hercules killing his family? _____

7. Hera was the mother of Hercules. True ☐ or false ☐?

8. Why was Hercules taught archery, wrestling and music? _____
   _____

9. Which other mythical hero was helped by Hercules? _____

10. Who was the father of Hercules? _____

11. What makes us think that Hercules might have forgiven Hera? _____
    _____

12. Use checks to give your opinion of the character of Hercules.

Trait	Not	Fairly	Very	Can't Tell	Reason for Answer
Brave					
Hot-tempered					
Cheerful					
Educated					
Adventurous					

13. Hercules was courageous and strong. Name other mythical characters who were courageous and strong and tell something about one of them.

   _____
   _____

Word Study

Find words in the story **similar** in meaning to:

1. poisonous _____
2. wed _____
3. brave _____
4. strife _____
5. transported _____

6. detested _____
7. went down _____
8. choked _____
9. insanity _____
10. skilled people _____

Narrative

Use these guidelines to write your own myth about an imaginary hero/heroine who performs amazing deeds.

1. The name and a description of your character.
2. When and where your legend takes place. (Long ago, the future.)
3. The problem your hero/heroine has to face.
4. How the problem is solved.
5. What was done by the people to show how grateful they were.

Activity

Color these pictures of monsters found in the legends of Hercules.

A Spearbird of the Marsh

Hydra

Geryon, the Three-Headed Giant

In Roman legends, Rome was built by Romulus and his twin

_____ (1) Remus along the banks of the Tiber

River. The Ancient Romans worshiped gods like Mercury, the

_____ (2) of the gods. _____ (3)

didn't worship Roman gods and were often slain or forced to

fight in shows for the poor called circuses. They could watch

chariot _____ (4), men fighting lions or fights to

the death between trained _____ (5) called

gladiators in the Colosseum, a huge arena whose

_____ (6) can still be seen in Rome.

The Romans were excellent, well-trained soldiers who

conquered many _____ (7), which then became

part of the Roman Empire. They used huge _____ (8) to hurl large boulders at the

walls of _____ (9) they attacked. They built long straight _____ (10)

so their armies could move quickly from place to place. Roman roads have been unearthed in

_____ (11), where Julius Caesar, a famous Roman general and

_____ (12), fought the Ancient Britons.

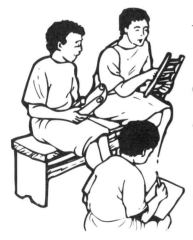

Ancient Rome had no government _____ (13).

Children were taught reading, math and writing in private schools

or at home by educated _____ (14) captured in other

lands. Unfortunately girls didn't have a long _____ (15),

as many were married before they were fifteen.

catapults	races	education	brother	roads
Britain	messenger	cities	slaves	ruins
emperor	countries	schools	warriors	Christians

1. Who was the brother of Romulus? _____

2. What was the war machine the Romans used to break down the walls of cities?

   _____

3. Children were taught in government schools in Ancient Rome. True ☐ or false ☐?

4. What does 'unearthed' mean? _____

5. Where have many old Roman roads been found? _____

6. What kind of people went to see the gladiators? _____

7. Romulus and Remus were similar in looks because _____

   _____

8. Check the sentence with which the writer would agree.

   (a) The Romans were friendly towards Christians. ☐

   (b) The Romans weren't good soldiers. ☐

   (c) Roman girls did not have a satisfactory education. ☐

9. On which river is Rome built? _____

10. Why did the Romans punish Christians? _____

    _____

11. What was the reason for building straight roads? _____

    _____

12. Using only information found in the story, match the pairs on the grid using checks.

	Fought in Circuses	Used as Teachers	Worshiped Jupiter	Worshiped Christ	Good Fighters
Romans					
Christians					
Educated slaves					
Gladiators					

13. Explain how circuses have changed since the days of Ancient Rome.

    _____

    _____

    _____

Language

Circle the correct **noun** to complete each sentence about the Romans.

1. Roman armies contained many (poets, farmers, sailors) who fought well to defend the land they owned.

2. Lands under efficient Roman (flags, gods, rule) soon prospered.

3. Slaves who pleased their masters could be freed to enjoy the same (rights, crimes, jails) as Roman citizens.

4. Britain's Roman roads ran north right up to (France, Scotland, Italy).

5. The Romans treated cruelly (friends, gods, enemies) who refused to surrender.

Procedure

Use the following guide to obtain facts for the chart.

1. Use the atlas index to find the page for each city.
2. Study this page to see if the city has a river and the country in which it is found.
3. Find the notes on the city in an encyclopedia and write an interesting point about it.
4. Use an atlas page to check whether the city is in the northern or southern hemisphere.

Ancient City	River	Country	Hemisphere	Interesting Point
Cairo				
Jerusalem				
Damascus				
Beijing				
Cape Town				
Rome				

Activity

Refer to your atlas and write the correct numbers against the cities on this network of ancient Roman roads in Britain. Roman names are in brackets.

☐ York (Eburacum)

☐ Gloucester (Glevum)

☐ London (Londinium)

☐ Chester (Deva)

☐ Winchester (Venta Belgarum)

☐ Leicester (Ratae)

☐ Lincoln (Lindum)

☐ St. Albans (Verulamlum)

☐ Bath (Aquae Sulis)

☐ Colchester (Camulodunum)

Humans have always used _____(1) ways of communicating. Primitive tribes drew pictures on cave walls and this _____(2) kind of written communication has been found in Spain, France and Australia. American Plains Indians used picture writing but, living on _____(3) land, also used smoke signals visible over _____(4) distances. African tribes in _____(5) jungles, where they couldn't see far, used drums. Long ago, _____(6) notches on message sticks or knots on string provided information carried by runners.

Army leaders have used carrier pigeons and navies developed a system of signaling with _____(7) flags called semaphore. Armies also used heliographs, which were mirrors that reflected the sun, to send long or _____(8) flashes of light. Helios was the sun-god in myths of the ancient Greeks who used _____(9) metal to reflect the sun's rays.

Now we have satellites, television, fax machines, _____(10) computer networks and the telephone invented by Bell in 1876. The invention of printing in the 15th century led to _____(11) books and newspapers.

Scientists using optical fibers the thickness of a _____(12) hair now send faster messages. Beams of light called lasers change the _____(13) signals of phone calls or TV pictures into light impulses. Lasers then send the light along _____(14) fibers over great distances without losing strength. At the receiving end, machines change the laser light back to the _____(15) message.

polished	carved	flat	original	worldwide
electrical	short	different	human	long
earliest	dense	colored	modern	glass

1. What did some African jungle tribes use to send messages? _____

2. In which countries have cave drawings been found? _____
_____

3. Check the sentence which tells us what the writer said.
   (a) Message sticks had knots on them. ☐
   (b) Cave drawings have been found in several countries. ☐
   (c) The Ancient Greeks used glass mirrors to reflect the sun. ☐

4. What were the benefits of polishing metal? _____
_____

5. American Plains Indians used smoke signals because _____
_____

6. What great 15th century invention improved communications? _____

7. Optic fibers are made of human hair. True ☐ or false ☐?

8. How did heliographs get their name? _____
_____

9. What was the first kind of written communication? _____
_____

10. What is the advantage of using laser beams? _____
_____

11. Why do you think cave pictures can still be seen after thousands of years?
_____

12. Write **fact** or **opinion** after each sentence.
    (a) Semaphore is the best method of communication. _____
    (b) Cave drawings have been found in France. _____
    (c) The telephone is the world's greatest invention. _____

13. How do you think communication will change in the future?
_____
_____

Grid

Check the information correctly on the grid below.

	carrier pigeons	polished metal	fax machines	flags	drums	smoke signals	pictures	phones	message sticks
navy									
Greeks									
modern peoples									
American Indians									
army									
cavemen									
African tribes									
runners									

Language

Circle the correct **adjectives** in each sentence about communication.

1. The Morse code using long and (silent, short, empty) sounds to send messages was invented by Samuel Morse in 1840.

2. Cave drawings recently found in Northern Australia are some of the world's (youngest, darkest, oldest) pictures.

3. In the 19th century, the Pony Express carried mail across (Antarctica, America, Germany).

4. People walking in the street can now receive calls on their (wooden, absent, mobile) phones.

5. Short faxed messages can be sent to (harmless, distant, written) countries in a few seconds.

Communication Activity

Communicate your own message to your partner after working out a code together (e.g. an alphabet code where a letter stands for another letter three places after it so that 'G' would stand for 'J' and 'Z' for 'C', etc.

Picture clues, as in a **rebus** could also be used (e.g. 🐝4 stands for 'before' or ☀💡 stands for 'sunlight' or ✋H stands for 'and').

Many scientists contributed to the development of television _____

_____(1) of the 20th century. One we remember is John Logie Baird, _____

_____(2), who gave the first public demonstration of

television in England in 1926 and color pictures

_____(3). Australian TV award

statuettes are named 'Logies'

_____(4).

To obtain television pictures, the light _____

_____(5) is taken in by a television camera

which then changes the light _____

_____(6). A microphone picks

up the sounds _____(7) and

changes those to electronic signals too. The camera's

'video' signals go _____

_____(8) and the microphone's 'audio' signals go to

a loudspeaker. These signals are picked up

_____(9) and our TV sets change the audio and video signals

_____(10) recorded by the camera and

microphone.

Many TV signals are transmitted _____(11) along electromagnetic

waves which travel at 300,000 km per second, the speed of light. Pictures sent this way can

only travel a distance of 250 kilometers. To send pictures _____

_____(12) other methods are used such as microwaves or satellites like

Telstar or Earlybird, launched in the 1960's.

Television links people around the world _____(13) and entertainment

and is also a valuable educational tool. However, there is a lot of criticism

_____ (14) about the sex and violence that can be watched

_____ (15) whose viewing habits are not supervised by parents.

through the air	two years later	by young people
from a scene	in the early years	into electronic signals
back to the original pictures	within communities	at the same time
to news items	to a picture tube	over greater distances
a Scottish engineer	by our antennas	in his honor

1. Which kind of signals go to a loudspeaker? _____

2. Baird showed colored TV pictures in 1928.   True ☐ or false ☐?

3. How fast do electromagnetic waves travel? _____

4. Explain how TV can be used as an educational tool. _____

   _____

5. A statuette is a small _____ .

6. What changes light into electronic signals? _____

7. Which Latin word in the story means 'related to vision'? _____

8. Check the sentence which tells us what the writer meant:
   (a) TV is an advantage if used properly. ☐
   (b) It's better to use electromagnetic waves over long distances. ☐
   (c) There should be more violent programs for young people. ☐

9. Use the numbers 1 to 3 to place the sentences in time order:
   (a) The first color TV pictures were shown in England. ☐
   (b) The satellite Telstar was launched. ☐
   (c) The first TV pictures were shown to the English public. ☐

10. How do we pick up electronic TV signals in our homes?

    _____

11. Why are satellites used to transmit TV programs?

    _____

12. Check the statement which tells us the main idea of paragraph four.
    (a) News items from around the world. ☐
    (b) Young people's programs. ☐
    (c) The advantages and disadvantages of TV. ☐
    (d) The violence on television. ☐

13. Television programs have changed greatly since TV first began in 1926. What types of programs do you expect to see in the year 2026?

    _____

    _____

Word Study

Find **synonyms** in the story for these words.

1. showing   _____
2. sent   _____
3. recall   _____
4. alter   _____
5. observed   _____

6. inside   _____
7. growth   _____
8. atmosphere _____
9. systems   _____
10. globe   _____

Chart - Use reference books in your library to complete the chart.

Invention	Inventor	Year	Country	Interesting Point
Diesel Engine				
Printing				
Telescope				
Jet Engine				
Telephone				
Airplane				
Pneumatic Tire				
Typewriter				
Dynamite				
Transistor				

Report

Think of all the great inventions in communication, transportation, medicine and science. Select one you would like to have invented and write about it using reference books.
Use these guidelines.

1. Name of the invention.
2. Name of the inventor and who he/she was.
3. When and where it was invented.
4. Description of the invention and how it is used.
5. Any problem faced during its development.
6. How important it is today.

The word dinosaur comes from two Greek words meaning '_____ (1) lizard'. They lived over 200 million years ago. Scientists learn about them by _____ (2) fossils, which are animal remains that have hardened into rock after millions of years under the _____ (3). People have found fossil dinosaur eggs and trace fossils which are often animal _____ (4) left in rock layers. When fossil bones are found they are covered with plaster or foam for _____ (5). We can also learn about dinosaurs by studying other _____ (6) land animals like elephants.

In 1822 an English doctor's _____ (7) found a large fossil tooth. She showed it to her husband, who _____ (8) fossils, and he realized it was a new kind of creature. Since then, remains have been discovered around the _____ (9). When found, fossil skeletons are carefully _____ (10) and then assembled on metal frames. Broken parts are repaired or replaced with pieces made from _____ (11), plaster or fiberglass.

Scientists do not know why dinosaurs _____ (12). One theory is that a giant asteroid hit the earth and raised huge _____ (13) of dust. These blocked out sunlight for several years and killed _____ (14). With no food for themselves or the animals they _____ (15), dinosaurs died too.

cleaned	ground	terrible	disappeared	ate
wife	collected	footprints	huge	clouds
world	plants	studying	protection	plastic

1. Check the sentence which tells us what the author said.

    (a) Scientists know why dinosaurs disappeared. ☐

    (b) Dinosaurs come from Greece. ☐

    (c) The doctor had not seen this kind of fossil before. ☐

2. What are the display frames made of? _____

3. What part of a dinosaur did the doctor's wife find? _____

4. In what year was the first dinosaur fossil found? _____

5. Check the statement which tells us the main idea of paragraph three.

    (a) The dangers from dust clouds. ☐

    (b) One suggestion for the disappearance of the dinosaurs. ☐

    (c) The plants eaten by dinosaurs. ☐

6. What blocked out the sun's rays? _____

7. Who first realized that dinosaurs had once lived on the earth? _____

    _____

8. Why is foam used? _____

9. In which country was a fossil tooth found? _____

10. What do we call footprints left in rocks? _____

11. Why do you think the skeleton parts are assembled on frames? _____

    _____

12. Write **fact** or **opinion** after each sentence.

    (a) Dinosaurs once lived on the Earth. _____

    (b) A giant asteroid wiped out all dinosaurs. _____

    (c) It is best to use plaster for repairs. _____

    (d) Dinosaur fossils have been discovered all over the world. _____

    (e) It is very important to study dinosaur fossils. _____

13. What would life be like today if dinosaurs were still alive? _____

    _____

    _____

Word Study

Find **antonyms** in the story for these words.

1. separated _____
2. soiled _____
3. lost _____
4. missed _____
5. tiny _____

6. softened _____
7. ignoring _____
8. lowered _____
9. carelessly _____
10. appeared _____

Report

Use reference books and write a report on the different ideas scientists have to explain how dinosaurs became extinct. Use these guidelines.

1. What kind of animals were dinosaurs?
2. When and where they lived.
3. Several different explanations for their disappearance.
4. Which theory (idea) you support and why.

Dinosaur Names

Tri-ocula-bi-pedi-saurus

Look how this imaginary dinosaur relates to its name. Use these Greek and Latin prefixes to make up your own imaginary dinosaur's name (e.g., Hexaheaded monodentidaurus). Draw it on a large piece of paper and color it.

Prefixes

bi (two)	uni (one)
mono (one)	duo (two)
tri (three)	quad (four)
hexa (six)	hepta (seven)
octa (eight)	deca (ten)
multi (many)	oculus (eye)
dentis (tooth)	nasus (nose)
pedis (foot)	digitus (toe)
auris (ear)	

Neptune, known as Poseidon to the Ancient Greeks, was the most important god of the sea in Roman _____ (1). The Romans believed he had _____ (2) over the seas and sailors who sailed them. They thought he could cause violent _____ (3), or prevent them to protect sailors. At Neptune festivals each July, Roman citizens feasted and drank _____ (4).

The Romans were a seafaring _____ (5) who imported many goods by ship so a sea god was important in their daily _____ (6). Sea travel was dangerous in those _____ (7) because of their small ships, so sailors often prayed to Neptune for protection.

Neptune was the son of _____ (8) and Ops. He married a sea nymph, a female spirit, and had a child called Triton who was half man and half _____ (9).

Artists often show Neptune carrying a three-pronged _____ (10), a hunting weapon popular with Mediterranean _____ (11). In some paintings, apart from the trident, he is shown carrying a _____ (12), to remind worshipers he is also the god of horses. Many _____ (13) have a statue of Neptune, including the Trevi fountain which is a popular tourist attraction in _____ (14).

The planet Neptune was named after this Roman god and its largest _____ (15) after Neptune's son.

fishermen	wine	Saturn	moon	people
myths	spear	Rome	times	power
storms	fountains	lives	fish	whip

1. What did the Greeks call their sea-god? _____

2. Where is the Trevi fountain? _____

3. What is a sea spirit called? _____

4. What does the word 'imported' mean? _____

   _____

5. What is the name given to a three-pronged spear? _____

6. Sailors didn't think Neptune could protect them. True ☐ or false ☐?

7. What was unusual about Triton? _____

   _____

8. Check the sentence which tells us what the author meant.
   (a) Triton was a fish. ☐
   (b) The Romans celebrate the god Neptune each year. ☐
   (c) Neptune was a Greek god. ☐

9. Who were the grandparents of Triton? _____

10. The planet Neptune's moon is called _____ .

11. Why was Neptune important to the Romans? _____

    _____

12. Many fountains include a statue of Neptune because _____

    _____

13. Do you think Neptune was seen as a good and fair god or a harsh and uncaring god? Explain your answer.

    _____

    _____

    _____

    _____

Word Study

Write **nouns** from the story which are described by these **adjectives**.

1.	female	_____	6.	violent	_____
2.	three-pronged	_____	7.	ancient	_____
3.	Roman	_____	8.	largest	_____
4.	popular	_____	9.	seafaring	_____
5.	important	_____	10.	daily	_____

Narrative

Write your own myth about an imaginary god or goddess. Use these guidelines.

1. The name of your god/goddess (of war, of thunder, of the sea).
2. When and where the story is set.
3. The problem the people want their god/goddess to solve.
4. The characters and events in your story.
5. The problem finally solved.

Grid

Use your library reference books to complete the chart below. One has been done for you.

Reference books used: _____

_____

God	Roman or Greek	Norse or Egyptian	Male or Female	God/Goddess of...	Book/Page No.
Neptune	Roman	-	Male	The Sea	
Mars					
Zeus					
Freyja					
Thor					
Aphrodite					
Osiris					
Diana					

In 1900 there were about 40,000 _____ (1) tigers in India. Now there are less

than 7,000 in the _____ (2) world. At a wildlife protection meeting of more than

one hundred nations in Florida in 1994, _____ (3) Asian countries, including

China and Japan, proposed greater protection for these _____ (4)

animals. Unfortunately, it is in these _____ (5) countries that 'Jinbou' is

widespread. This is the ancient belief that taking medicines prepared from animal parts will

improve _____ (6) health.

Almost all parts of the tiger are used: the eyes for

malaria or fever in _____ (7) children; its

whiskers for toothache; tiger bone preparations

for _____ (8) joints; its teeth for

asthma; its fat for vomiting and

_____ (9) dog bites and its tail for

skin diseases. Its beautiful _____ (10)

coat was once popular for rugs but import

bans on such items mean

_____ (11) poachers often leave

the skins and take the more _____ (12)

parts for use in oriental medicines. This very _____ (13) trade has been worth

billions of dollars in _____ (14) years.

Let us hope you still have the opportunity to see tigers roaming wild in

_____ (15) jungles when you are an adult.

poor	painful	magnificent	tropical	aching
profitable	Asian	entire	young	striped
cruel	ten	recent	valuable	wild

1. Where was the wildlife protection meeting held? _____

2. Which country had thousands of tigers at the start of this century? _____

3. Match the information correctly on the grid below. Some have been done for you.

Tiger Part	Rugs	Malaria	Dog bites	Toothache	Skin disease	Fever	Asthma	Vomiting	Aching joints
Eyes						✔			
Whiskers									
Bone									
Teeth									
Fat			✔						
Tail									
Coat									

4. What does the word 'recent' mean? _____

5. What is 'Jinbou'? _____

6. Check the sentence with which the writer would agree.

    (a) It would be nice to see tigers in the wild in the 21st century. ☐

    (b) Tiger parts should be used in all parts of the world. ☐

    (c) Tiger skin rugs look nice in a lounge room. ☐

7. There are only 7,000 tigers left in India today. True ☐ or false ☐?

8. Why has poaching been so profitable? _____

    _____

9. What would have been the aim of the Florida meeting? _____

10. Tiger skin rugs are not sold now because _____

    _____

11. Why would it be difficult to stop trade in tiger parts for Asian medicines? _____

    _____

12. Why do you think people bought tiger rugs? _____

    _____

13. How would you help to save the last tigers in the wild? _____

    _____

    _____

    _____

Word Study

Find words in the story **similar** in meaning to:

1. whole _____   6. wandering _____

2. nearly _____   7. embargoes _____

3. suggested _____   8. ailments _____

4. countries _____   9. vicious _____

5. fewer _____   10. chance _____

Language

Circle one **adjective** to make each sentence correct.

1. Hunters once shot tigers on (clever, cheap, expensive) safari expeditions.

2. Using animal parts also threatens other (dead, wild, tame) animal species.

3. Clearing (empty, dense, friendly) jungles destroys the homes of tigers.

4. Though it is banned, the (illegal, lawful, wise) tiger trade continues.

5. Rhinoceroses are also threatened with extinction by the (untidy, new, ancient) medicine trade.

Writing

Imagine you are a tiger in the jungles of India.
Tell how you were hunted by poachers and what happened.
Use these guidelines.

1. Who you are.

2. What you look like.

3. Where you live.

4. When the poachers appeared in your area.

5. Why they were after you.

6. What happened during the hunt.

7. Why you are still alive to tell your story.

8. Your advice for other tigers.

Early powered carriages were _____ (1) by steam. In 1885 German engineers,

Daimler and Benz, _____ (2) the first successful gasoline-driven cars. These

engines _____ (3) power when a mixture of fuel and air _____ (4)

inside the engine. Early electric cars were quiet and pollution free but their batteries had to be

_____ (5) after about 50 km.

Road safety regulations were _____ (6) in 1865 and someone had to walk in

front of any self-propelled carriage with a red flag or a red lantern to _____ (7)

pedestrians.

The first cars were _____ (8) by hand

by skilled craftsmen, but Henry Ford wanted

affordable cars and developed an assembly line in

1914. Workers _____ (9) on either side of

a moving belt and _____ (10) the different

parts to the

T-model Ford chassis as it passed by. Today, in many countries, robots have

_____ (11) these workers on assembly lines.

The electric starter replaced starting handles, and pneumatic tires with their cushion of air

_____ (12) rides more comfortable. Safety glass that didn't _____ (13)

into dangerous splinters was introduced in the 1920's.

More streamlined solar-powered or electric cars of the future will reduce the danger from

lead or benzene in the air we _____ (14). Cars have changed our lifestyle but

_____ (15) thousands of people on the world's roads each year.

shatter	gain	replaced	breathe	developed
explodes	driven	made	stood	kill
recharged	warn	added	built	passed

1. Safety glass was a big advantage because _____

   _____

2. Why did a person carry a red flag? _____

3. Which country did Benz come from? _____

4. What does it mean to be 'skilled'? _____

   _____

5. Use the numbers 1 to 5 and number these events in time order.

   (a) The assembly line. ☐   **(d)** Road safety regulations in Britain. ☐

   (b) Robots in car factories. ☐   **(e)** First cars to use gasoline. ☐

   (c) Invention of safety glass. ☐

6. Henry Ford used an assembly line to make expensive cars. True ☐ or false ☐?

7. What was the main problem with electric cars? _____

   _____

8. Check the sentence with which the writer would agree.

   (a) All cars should use leaded gasoline. ☐

   (b) Cars are an advantage and a problem. ☐

   (c) Early electric cars were perfect. ☐

9. Why were early cars so expensive? _____

10. What are the two main problems with modern cars? _____

    _____

11. Which word in the story means 'containing air'? _____

12. Name one way in which cars have changed our lifestyle. _____

    _____

13. How would life be different today without cars? _____

    _____

Language

Circle the correct **verb** to complete each sentence about cars.

1. Many farmers (lifted, hated, designed) the first noisy, smelly cars.

2. Engines (using, finding, selling) gasoline are called internal combustion engines.

3. By 1903 cars could (stop, spin, travel) at just over 30 km/h.

4. Passengers were (taken, exposed, treated) to bad weather in early cars.

5. Some owners of private roads asked drivers for higher fees because they thought the first cars (built, ordered, damaged) the surfaces of their roads.

Exposition

Many road accidents happen at night because certain car colors are difficult to see. Give details to support a suggestion that all cars should be yellow or white. Use these guidelines.

1. Statement of the road accidents problem.

2. Introducing the suggestion (laws, newspaper debate, advertising, etc.)

3. Evidence supporting the idea (yellow/white paint reflects the most light, less of a problem for the color-blind).

4. Any arguments against the idea.

5. Final statements of support for the suggestion.

Activity

Look at these old style cars and design one of your own.

An English fleet of eleven ships carried the _____ (1) British convicts to Australia, setting sail from Portsmouth in May, 1787, under Captain Arthur Phillip in his flagship 'Sirius'. Over 700 _____ (2) convicts were carried below decks in _____ (3) ships called transports. The fleet also carried children, soldiers and animals.

Phillip took fruit and vegetables to prevent scurvy, a _____ (4) disease which killed thousands of sailors. Green vegetables were also grown on board on _____ (5) strips of cloth. The Canary Islands, Rio de Janeiro and Cape Town were three _____ (6) ports of call on the difficult voyage to Botany Bay. There they picked up _____ (7) water, food and animals and repaired damage caused in _____ (8) storms.

Phillip and his advance party didn't think Botany Bay would make a _____ (9) settlement. Fresh water was _____ (10) and the soil was too poor to grow crops to support a _____ (11) colony. The bay was open to the sea, so strong winds could be _____ (12) for ships.

Phillip sailed north up the coast and found the _____ (13) Port Jackson harbor where Sydney stands today. The tank stream in Sydney Cove provided water, and _____ (14) water up to the shore made it easy to unload ships. Phillip then claimed the _____ (15) coast for Britain on January 26, 1788.

dangerous	east	miserable	welcome	new
deep	first	terrible	violent	leaky
magnificent	damp	suitable	fresh	scarce

1. Which disease killed thousands of sailors? _____

2. Which plants were grown on board the ships? _____

3. Is Botany Bay north or south of Sydney Cove? _____

4. Check the sentence which tells us what the writer said.

    (a) The fleet carried only convicts. ☐
    (b) Phillip lost thousands of sailors on the voyage. ☐
    (c) The fleet was caught in storms. ☐

5. What were transports used for? _____

6. Give **two** reasons why Botany Bay was not chosen as the site for a new colony.

    (a) _____

    (b) _____

7. Seven hundred people sailed on the first fleet. True ☐ or false ☐?

8. Check the statement which tells us the main idea of paragraph three.

    (a) The growing of crops. ☐
    (b) Exploring the coast. ☐
    (c) The problems of Botany Bay. ☐

9. The first fleet took about (3 months, 8 weeks, 2 years, 8 months) to reach Australia.

10. Why did the writer say '...welcome ports of call...'? _____

    _____

11. Which word in the story describes
    the poor condition of some of the ships? _____

12. Write **fact** or **opinion** after each sentence below.

    (a) Scurvy was a problem on early voyages. _____

    (b) The fleet should have carried fewer children. _____

    (c) Port Jackson is the world's finest harbor. _____

13. How do you think the first convicts felt when they finally saw the shores of Australia?

    _____

    _____

Language

Circle the correct **adjective** to complete each sentence about the first fleet.

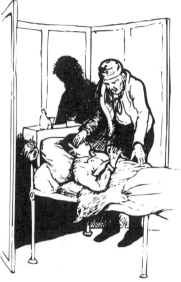

1. Only 23 convicts died on the (short, happy, difficult) voyage.

2. Records show the convicts were treated badly by some (kind, friendly, cruel) officers and marines.

3. Many crew members of the 'Friendship' died of scurvy on the (outward, return, weak) journey to England.

4. The fleet carried horses, goats, cattle, pigs and sheep among the (domesticated, wild, useless) animals aboard.

5. Cape Town was the (only, last, first) main port of call on the voyage to Australia.

Brainstorming

Imagine you are colonists sailing off to settle in a new land. Write on a chart all the necessary things you would need to find at a site for a new settlement. Use these guidelines.

Things which would help to start a successful settlement (e.g. fresh water).

Things to avoid when judging the merits of a new site (e.g. hostile inhabitants).

After the ideas are written on the chart, write down what you think are the three most important ones.

(1) _____

_____

(2) _____

_____

(3) _____

_____

Report

Read about the disease **scurvy** which took the lives of thousands of sailors on long voyages in those times. Write a report about it. Use these guidelines.

1. What a person with scurvy looked like.   **2.**   Why people got the disease.

3. What happened to people with scurvy.   **4.**   How some leaders prevented it.

5. Whether it is a problem today and why.

Spring is a _____ (1) that many like best,

When all naked trees begin to show _____ (2),

Birds _____ (3) twigs to build a nest,

Migrating swallows – _____ (4) have they been?

Nights grow _____ (5), warmer days,

Baseball bats swung by _____ (6) in white,

No discomfort from a _____ (7) sun's rays,

Daffodils in garden beds, a _____ (8) sight!

The morning quiet _____ (9) by machines on lawns,

Houses spring cleaned, the _____ (10) done,

Bright red sunsets and glowing _____ (11),

Everyone's _____ (12) for winter's now gone.

Freshly painted boats glide on _____ (13) seas,

The bleating of _____ (14) as they frolic in the lea,

Brightly-colored _____ (15) compete with the bees,

Spring is alive for the world to see!

happy	where	time	hot	shorter
broken	smooth	lambs	colorful	dawns
washing	green	players	gather	butterflies

1. The nights are longer in spring than in winter. True ☐ or false ☐?

2. Give your own word for 'glide' as used in the poem. _____

3. What does the writer mean by 'smooth seas'? _____

4. What is the noise made by the lambs? _____

5. What do you think the machines are in verse three? _____

6. The 'players in white' are ball players and not umpires because _____

_____

7. Without using your dictionary, what do you think daffodils are? _____

8. Check the sentence with which the writer would agree.
   (a) Everyone likes spring the best. ☐
   (b) The sun in spring is too hot during the day. ☐
   (c) Spring is a wonderful time. ☐

9. What does the writer mean by 'naked trees'? _____

10. Give the word in the poem which is a field or meadow. _____

11. What do you think the writer meant by 'butterflies compete with the bees'?

_____

12. Use the numbers 1 to 8 to order the things **you** like best about spring.

    (a) warmer days ☐   (e) busy bees ☐

    (b) new leaves on trees ☐   (f) shorter nights ☐

    (c) lambs bleating ☐   (g) brightly-colored butterflies ☐

    (d) baseball ☐   (h) birds building nests ☐

13. Describe the things you like about spring.

_____

_____

_____

Word Study

Find words in the poem which are **synonyms** for these words.

1. shining   _____

2. play   _____

3. silence   _____

4. disappeared   _____

5. construct   _____

6. move smoothly   _____

7. observe   _____

8. period   _____

9. display   _____

10. delighted   _____

Report

Write a report on spring using the following guidelines.
1. Opening sentence describing the seasons.
2. Using the poem, describe some of the things that happen in nature in spring.
3. Using the poem, describe some of the things people do in spring.
4. Closing sentence about your thoughts on spring when comparing it with the other seasons.

Poetic Text

Brainstorm words which describe your favorite season.

_____

Write your own four-line poem about one of the seasons. Use the same rhyming pattern as the poem about spring, e.g., lines 1 and 3 rhyme, lines 2 and 4 rhyme.

_____

_____

_____

Florence Nightingale was born in 1820 of wealthy British parents living in Florence, Italy, but spent her _____(1) in England. Her parents were horrified when she became a nurse, as nursing in those _____(2) was not a respected profession. Later, she was asked to take a _____(3) of nurses to the Crimea in 1854 where _____(4) and France were fighting Russia.

In Scutari they found over 5,000 sick and wounded men and a filthy _____(5) infested with rats. She and her nurses improved _____(6) so much that very few _____(7) died from then on. Florence regularly checked the wounded at night and became known as 'the lady with the _____(8)'. She improved hospital treatment for ordinary soldiers who were not _____(9).

After the Crimean War she refused all _____(10) and honors. The public donated large sums of _____(11) because of her work in the war and she used it to begin the Nightingale Training _____(12) for nurses in London.

An _____(13) she had caught during the war made her an invalid and she gradually became blind. In 1907 she became the first _____(14) to be awarded the Order of Merit by a British government. She died in London in 1910 after a _____(15) of caring for others.

School	group	life	conditions	medals
childhood	hospital	woman	officers	days
patients	illness	money	lamp	Britain

1. Who helped Britain fight Russia? _____

2. Which animals were a danger to the patients in the hospital? _____

3. Florence's parents were glad when she became a nurse. True ☐ or false ☐?

4. Why did Florence carry a lamp? _____
_____

5. How old was Florence when she went to Scutari? _____

6. Florence was probably called Florence because _____
_____

7. Which honor did Florence finally accept? _____

8. Use checks to give your opinion of Florence's character.

Trait	Not	Fairly	Very	Can't Tell	Reason for Answer
Caring					
Selfish					
Modest					
Generous					
Comical					

9. How old was Florence when she died? _____

10. What do you think Florence and her nurses did to improve hospital conditions?
_____

11. What happened when the nurses improved conditions at the hospital? _____
_____

12. Check the sentence with which the writer would agree.

    (a) Florence did not look after ordinary soldiers. ☐

    (b) Nursing was a respected profession when Florence became a nurse. ☐

    (c) Florence Nightingale led a worthwhile life. ☐

13. Explain Florence Nightingale's reaction if she were to visit today's hospitals.
_____
_____

Word Study

Find **antonyms** in the passage for these words.

1. accepted _____

2. pleased _____

3. quickly _____

4. spotless _____

5. poor _____

6. adulthood _____

7. many _____

8. lost _____

9. peace _____

10. healthy _____

Language

Circle the correct **noun** to complete each sentence.

1. Florence Nightingale was the (matron, pioneer, president) of the nursing profession as we know it today.

2. Florence's family's initial disapproval of her chosen profession almost prevented her from working in (convents, schools, hospitals).

3. During the Crimean War, the British secretary asked Florence to take charge of (supplies, nursing, artillery).

4. Florence Nightingale introduced hygienic methods of nursing in (war time, medieval time, peace time).

5. Graduates of the Nightingale Training School for (nurses, doctors, therapists) traveled to all parts of the world to teach nursing.

Narrative

Imagine you are a helper or soldier in Scutari hospital when Florence and her nurses arrive. Write a narrative about what is happening around you, using these guidelines.

1. Describe how you came to be at the hospital.

2. Use your imagination and describe the conditions at the hospital.

3. Describe what Florence and her nurses did to improve the conditions.

4. Describe the feelings of the soldiers towards 'the lady with the lamp'.

5. Describe what happened to you when the war ended.

England's great novelist Charles Dickens _____(1) *Oliver Twist*, a story of life in 19th century London slums. It's about a boy whose mother _____(2) in a workhouse for the poor after giving birth to Oliver. At nine he _____(3) work at another children's workhouse. Because he worked hard he was hungry so he _____(4) more food and for his impudence he was _____(5). He was also badly treated by another young worker.

Later, Oliver ran away to London. There he _____(6) Jack Dawkins, the 'Artful Dodger', who _____(7) him to Fagin, a cruel old man who had _____(8) a gang of young pickpockets. Soon he left Fagin's house but Bill Sykes and his girlfriend Nancy, Fagin's friends, _____(9) him to go back.

Eventually Oliver _____(10) that Sykes had killed Nancy and some time later had accidentally _____(11) himself. Fagin had been _____(12) to be hanged and Jack _____(13) for his crimes. Oliver was _____(14) by the kind, rich Mr. Brownlow and they lived happily in a small country village.

Dickens wrote his novel to bring attention to the wretched lives _____(15) by poor people in the workhouses and slum areas of London.

requested	led	hanged	dies	organized
forced	adopted	met	wrote	sentenced
began	introduced	heard	imprisoned	punished

1. In which city is the story set? _____

2. Who was known as the 'Artful Dodger'? _____

3. Who adopted Oliver? _____

4. What does the word 'impudence' mean? _____

   _____

5. Why was Oliver so hungry that he asked for more food?

   _____

6. Oliver's mother died when he was born. True ☐ or false ☐?

7. Oliver ran away to London because _____

   _____

8. Is *Oliver Twist* a true story? Explain. _____

   _____

9. Which word tells us Oliver didn't want to go back to Fagin's gang? _____

10. Why do you think Jack took Oliver to meet Fagin? _____

    _____

11. Check the sentence which tells us what the writer meant.
    (a) Bill Sykes was a friend to Oliver. ☐
    (b) Oliver wouldn't enjoy a better life with Mr. Brownlow. ☐
    (c) Dickens was a friend of the poor. ☐

12. Why do you think Sykes took Oliver back to the gang? _____

    _____

13. Do you think this novel had any effect on the lives of the poor people in the slum areas of London?

    _____

    _____

    _____

Word Study

Find words in the story which are **similar** in meaning to:

1. put in prison   _____

2. a writer   _____

3. merciless   _____

4. insolence   _____

5. thieves   _____

6. cunning   _____

7. compeled   _____

8. dwelt   _____

9. miserable   _____

10. districts   _____

Grid

Use checks to match the pairs in the grid. Only use information from the story.

	Dickens	Oliver's mother	Fagin	Oliver	Sykes	Mr. Brownlow	Jack
Kind							
Rich							
Poor							
Cruel							
Hardworking							
Criminal							

Fagin's gang of young pickpockets were being trained to steal from people. Use these guidelines to support an argument that stealing is wrong.

1. Opening sentence – stealing is wrong and why.

2. Give examples of the bad effect on victims of crime, for example a school friend or neighbor.

3. Explanation of certain examples where one can understand the reasons for theft (e.g. a poor parent stealing a toy for a child at Christmas). Is it still wrong?

4. A final statement explaining how you think this problem with children and adults can be dealt with in schools.

There are two kinds of deserts, _____(1), both are dry. The few people living in or near deserts are often nomads seeking pasture _____ _____(2) or oases, where water is regularly available, just as their ancestors have done _____(3).

Desert rainfall is unreliable and droughts can last _____(4). Temperatures often reach 40°C during the day but can plunge to freezing _____(5) under clear skies. Insects bring sand fly fever, the eye disease trachoma spread _____(6) and malaria from mosquitoes which breed _____(7). The hot sun bakes the ground dry, then dust storms blow away the valuable topsoil used to grow food _____(8) of deserts.

_____(9), particularly by goats, the destruction _____(10) and poor farming methods some desert regions are spreading, so scientists have to work harder to improve the situation.

_____(11), like Algeria and Saudi Arabia, scientists have reduced areas of desert. They pumped in water _____(12) using solar-powered water pumps, and enriched the soil together with improved farming methods. These improvements have led to increases _____(13). Unfortunately, the wealth obtained from the sale of new crops _____(14) has not reached the ordinary desert people, who still live _____(15) in this harsh environment.

in the oases	for their animals	in some desert populations	for centuries
in poverty	by flies	over long distances	at night
In richer countries	for years	like cotton	hot or cold
of trees	on the edges	Because of overgrazing	

1. What blows away valuable topsoil? _____

2. Which animals damage desert environments? _____

3. Which desert eye disease is spread by flies? _____

4. Check the sentence which tells us what the author said.
   (a) The ordinary desert people are wealthy. ☐
   (b) Dust storms can blow away the best soil. ☐
   (c) Rain falls regularly in cold deserts. ☐

5. What is meant by 'overgrazing'? _____
   _____

6. Desert people could improve their poor soils by using (shade the correct answers):

rocks	fertilizers	water	animal manure	oil	insects	sand

7. What is the name given to desert wanderers? _____

8. Check the statement which tells us the main idea of paragraph two.
   (a) High temperatures in desert regions. ☐
   (b) Growing food in deserts. ☐
   (c) The problems found in deserts. ☐

9. Explain 'rainfall is unreliable' in your own words. _____
   _____

10. The day's heat escapes quickly into the air because _____
    _____

11. Where have most improvements been made? _____

12. Write **fact** or **opinion** after each of these sentences.
    (a) Desert nights are usually cold. _____
    (b) Water is found in oases. _____
    (c) Desert people should live somewhere else. _____
    (d) Deserts are the worst places to live. _____

13. Design a village that would be self-sufficient in the desert. Write a description.
    _____
    _____

Report

Write a report on deserts using these guidelines.

1. Define what a desert is and how deserts are formed.
2. Describe the different kinds of deserts.
3. Describe the weather conditions in deserts.
4. The kinds of animals which live there.
5. Describe the lives of the people who live there.
6. What has been done to overcome problems for people living in deserts.
7. Final comment on your thoughts about living in a desert.

Ordering Preferences

Number these desert problems in order with the one you dislike most as number one.
Write a sentence to explain why you chose this order.

☐ high temperatures   ☐ dust storms   _____

☐ malarial mosquitoes   ☐ scarce water   _____

☐ poverty   ☐ deforestation   _____

☐ long droughts   ☐ freezing nights   _____

☐ sand fly fever   ☐ poor soils   _____

☐ trachoma   ☐ overgrazing   _____

Map Exercise

Use your atlas to put the correct numbers by these deserts of the world.

☐ Sahara Desert
☐ Arabian Desert
☐ Great Sandy Desert
☐ Thar Desert
☐ Gobi Desert
☐ Atacama Desert
☐ Somali Desert
☐ Kalahari Desert
☐ Mojave Desert
☐ Namib Desert

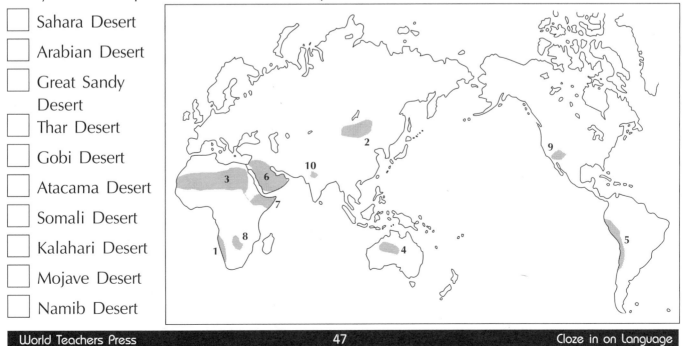

The surface of the Earth is made up of _____ (1) like those on an onion. We live on the crust which _____ (2) on a deep layer called a mantle. The mantle is almost 3,000 km thick and is mostly hot _____ (3) rock formed by the intense heat inside the _____ (4). Many scientists believe the crust is _____ (5) up into tectonic plates with cracks around their edges. _____ (6) mostly occur along these fault lines when plates _____ (7) as they float on the mantle. Sometimes, following a major shock, there are several _____ (8) tremors called aftershocks. A strong undersea earthquake can cause _____ (9) waves called tsunamis to sweep ashore and _____ (10) thousands of people. Severe damage is usual at the _____ (11), the surface area directly above the earthquake.

Some great cities have been _____ (12) by earthquakes with great loss of life as in Tokyo in 1923. In China in 1556 an _____ (13) 830,000 people died and in 1976 many more thousands lost their lives.

Improved building designs mean some modern skyscrapers can visibly _____ (14) but not be damaged because of the materials used in their _____ (15).

continent   ocean   continent   ocean   continent

plate   plate   plate

1. What is the hot liquid rock below the earth's surface called? _____

2. Human beings live on the earth's crust. True ☐ or false ☐?

3. What are giant waves caused by earthquakes called? _____

4. What does the word 'intense' mean? _____

_____

5. Which country suffered an earthquake in the 16th century? _____

6. Use the numbers 1 to 4 to place these events in time order:

   (a) People in coastal villages drown. ☐   (b) Tsunamis sweep to shore. ☐

   (c) Plates float on the mantle. ☐   (d) Tectonic plates collide. ☐

7. What can cause tsunamis? _____

8. What changes rock into liquid rock? _____

9. Tectonic plates collide because _____

_____

10. What are the cracks around the plates called? _____

11. Why do people still have to be careful after a strong quake? _____

_____

12. Write **fact** or **opinion** after each sentence:

    (a) It is hot at the center of the earth. _____

    (b) Earthquakes are worse than wars. _____

    (c) Tokyo was damaged by an earthquake. _____

    (d) Tsunamis are waves. _____

13. How do you think you would you react in the event of a tsunami?

_____

_____

_____

Word Study

Find **synonyms** in the story for the following words.

1. powerful   _____
2. rims   _____
3. happen   _____
4. badly damaged   _____
5. fluid   _____

6. crash violently _____
7. fierce   _____
8. enormous   _____
9. perished   _____
10. move to and fro _____

Character Self-Portrait

Read some reference materials or watch a video about the world's worst earthquake disasters. For example, the Tokyo earthquake of 1923, San Francisco 1906, Mexico City 1985 or Kobe 1994. Your teacher may help you to find information on these earthquakes.

Now imagine that you are a survivor of one of these earthquakes. After discussing (in small groups) what it would have been like to be in an earthquake, complete the form letter below.

I am	
I lived	
I used to	
One day I	
Now I	
Soon I	
Then I	
I hated	
I only hope	

Explanation

Use the modeled writing method below to write an explanation of earthquakes.

1. Earthquakes are _____

2. They occur because _____

3. The damage they cause includes _____

4. Aftershocks are _____

5. Some of the worst earthquakes were in _____

6. Architects can improve safety by _____

7. If an earthquake struck here I _____

PAGE 6 Edward Jenner - Cloze

1. by a virus
2. in the air
3. for life
4. centuries ago
5. In some wars
6. to N. America
7. with liquid
8. A British doctor
9. from smallpox
10. a mild cattle disease
11. from a dairymaid's sore
12. on the boy
13. In 1967
14. in a laboratory

PAGE 7 - Comprehension

1. A virus
2. vacca
3. false
4. 1796
5. vaccination
6. Britain
7. 171 years
8. (b)
9. (d), (b), (c), (a)
10. No
11. More soldiers died from smallpox than fighting
12. Answers may vary.

PAGE 8 - Activities

Activities

1. mild
2. liquid
3. eliminate
4. laboratory
5. dangerous
6. disease
7. experiment
8. discovered
9. settlers
10. fight/fighting

Semantic Grid

	malaria	penicillin	aspirin	smallpox	polio	x-rays	leprosy	antiseptics
C. Gerhardt			✓					
A. Fleming		✓						
J. Lister								✓
E. Jenner				✓				
Father Damien							✓	
R.Ross	✓							
J. Salk					✓			
R. Roentgen						✓		

Group Discussion

Answers may vary.

PAGE 9 Hercules - Cloze

1. Roman
2. strong
3. hated
4. cradle
5. young
6. music
7. madness
8. serve
9. Hydra
10. arrows
11. descended
12. guarding
13. search
14. carried
15. daughter

Page 10 - Comprehension

1. He killed his family
2. 12 years
3. A three-headed watchdog
4. killed violently
5. (b)
6. Hera
7. false
8. To give him a rounded education, but answers may vary.
9. Jason
10. Zeus
11. He married her daughter
12. Hercules' character trait table

Trait	Not	Fairly	Very	Can't Tell	Reason for answer
Brave			✓		Answers Vary
Hot-tempered			✓		Killed his family
Cheerful				✓	Doesn't say
Educated		✓			Taught by experts
Adventurous			✓		Went with Jason

Page 11 - Activities

Word Study

1. venomous
2. married
3. courageous
4. trouble
5. carried
6. hated
7. descended
8. strangled
9. madness
10. experts

Narrative

Answers may vary.

Activity

Teacher check.

PAGE 12 The Romans - Cloze

1. brother
2. messenger
3. Christians
4. races
5. warriors
6. ruins
7. countries
8. catapults
9. cities
10. roads
11. Britain
12. emperor
13. schools
14. slaves
15. education

PAGE 13 - Comprehension

1. Remus
2. a catapult
3. false
4. to dig up or uncover
5. Britain
6. poor people
7. they were twins
8. (c)
9. Tiber
10. They did not worship Roman gods
11. To move armies quickly
12. Romans = worshiped Jupiter, good fighters
   Christians = fought in circuses, worshiped Christ
   E/Slaves = used as teachers,
   Gladiators = fought in circuses, good fighters

PAGE 14 - Activities

Language

1. farmers
2. rule
3. rights
4. Scotland
5. enemies

Procedure

Ancient City	River	Country	Hemisphere	Interesting Point
London	Thames	England	Northern	Answers vary
New York	Hudson	USA	Northern	
Cairo	Nile	Egypt	Northern	
Jerusalem	—	Israel	Northern	
Damascus	Barada	Syria	Northern	
Beijing	Tonghui	China	Northern	
Capetown	—	S. Africa	Southern	
Rome	Tiber	Italy	Northern	

Activity

1 = London (Londinium)
2 = Colchester (Camulodunum)
3 = St. Albans (Verulamlum)
4 = Winchester (Venta Bulgarium)
5 = Bath (Aquae Sulis)
6 = Gloucester (Glevum)
7 = Leicester (Ratae)
8 = Lincoln (Lindum)
9 = Chester (Deva)
10 = York (Eburacum)

PAGE 15 Communications History

1. different
2. earliest
3. flat
4. long
5. dense
6. carved
7. colored
8. short
9. polished
10. worldwide
11. modern
12. human
13. electrical
14. glass
15. original

PAGE 16 - Comprehension

1. drums
2. Australia, Spain and France
3. (b)
4. Answers may vary.
5. They lived on flat land.
6. printing
7. false
8. from the sun-god Helios
9. pictures on cave walls
10. Answers may vary.
11. protected from the elements
12. (a) opinion (b) fact (c) opinion

PAGE 17 - Activities

Grid

	carrier pigeons	polished metal	tax machines	flags	drums	smoke signals	pictures	phones	message sticks
navy					✓				
Greeks		✓							
modern peoples			✓					✓	
American Indians						✓	✓		
army	✓								
cavemen							✓		
African tribes					✓				
runners									✓

Language

1. short
2. oldest
3. America
4. mobile
5. distant

Communication Activity
Answers may vary.

PAGE 18 Television - *Cloze*

1. in the early years
2. a Scottish engineer
3. two years later
4. in his honor   5. from a scene
6. into electronic signals
7. at the same time
8. to a picture tube
9. by our antennas
10. back to the original pictures
11. through the air
12. over greater distances
13. to news items
14. within communities
15. by young people

PAGE 19 - *Comprehension*

1. Audio
2. true 1.3 300,000 km /sec
3. Answers may vary.
4. statue
5. the television camera
6. video   7. (a)
8. (a) 2 (b) 3 (c) 1
9. with our TV antennas
10. to send TV pictures over greater distances
11. (c)

PAGE 20 - *Activities*

Word Study
1. demonstration   2. transmitted
3. remember   4. change
5. watched   6. within
7. development   8. air
9. methods   10. world

Invention	Inventor	Year	Country	Interesting Point	
Diesel engine	R. Diesel	1894	Germany		A n s w e r s v a r y
Printing	J. Gutenberg	c. 1440	Germany		
Telescope	Galileo	1609	Italy		
Jet engine	Frank Whittle	1941	England		
Telephone	A.G. Bell	1876	USA		
Aeroplane	Wright Brothers	1903	USA		
Pneumatic tyre	R.Thomson	1845	Scotland		
Typewriter	C. Sholes	1867	USA		
Dynamite	A. Nobel	1867	Sweden		
Transistor	J. Barden W. Bratten W. Shockley	1947	USA		

Report
Teacher check.

PAGE 21 Dinosaurs - *Cloze*

1. terrible   2. studying
3. ground   4. footprints
5. protection   6. huge
7. wife   8. collected
9. world   10. cleaned

11. plastic   12. disappeared
13. clouds   14. plants
15. ate

PAGE 22 - *Comprehension*

1. (c)   2. metal
3. tooth   4. 1822
5. (b)   6. clouds of dust
7. an English doctor
8. to prevent damage to fossil bones
9. England   10. trace fossils
11. Answers may vary.
12. (a) fact (b) opinion (c) opinion
    (d) fact (e) opinion

PAGE 23 - *Activities*

1. assembled   2. cleaned
3. found   4. hit
5. giant/huge   6. hardened
7. studying   8. raised
9. carefully   10. disappeared

Report
Answers may vary.

Dinosaur names
Teacher check

PAGE 24 Neptune - *Cloze*

1. myths   2. power
3. storms   4. wine
5. people   6. lives
7. times   8. Saturn
9. fish   10. spear
11. fishermen   12. whip
13. fountains   14. Rome
15. moon

PAGE 25 - *Comprehension*

1. Poseidon   2. Rome
3. sea nymph
4. to bring in from a foreign country
5. trident   6. false
7. he was half man half fish
8. (b)
9. Saturn and Ops 10. Triton
11. the sea played an important part in their lives
12. he is associated with water

PAGE 26 - *Activities*

Word Study
1. spirit   2. spear
3. god/citizens/myths
4. weapon/fountain
5. god   6. storms
7. Greeks   8. moon
9. people   10. lives

Narrative
Answers may vary.

Chart

	Roman or Greek	Norse or Egyptian	Male or Female	God/Goddess of....	Page Number
Neptune	Roman	——	Male	The sea	p.178
Mars	Roman	——	Male	War	A n s w e r s v a r y
Zeus	Greek	——	Male	The sky	
Freyja	——	Norse	Female	Love & beauty	
Thor	——	Norse	Male	Thunder & lightning	
Aphrodite	Greek	——	Female	Love	
Osiris	——	Egyptian	Male	Underworld	
Diana	Roman	——	Female	Hunting	

PAGE 27 The Tiger - *Cloze*

1. wild   2. entire   3. ten
4. magnificent   5. Asian
6. poor   7. young
8. aching   9. painful
10. striped   11. cruel
12. valuable   13. profitable
14. recent   15. tropical

PAGE 28 - *Comprehension*

1. Florida   2. India
3. Match the pairs grid

Tiger Part	Rugs	Malaria	Dog Bites	Toothache	Skin disease	Fever	Asthma	Vomiting	Aching joints
Eyes		✓				✓			
Whiskers			✓						
Bone									✓
Teeth									
Fat		✓						✓	
Tail						✓			
Coat	✓								

4. of late occurrence, not long past; answers may vary.
5. The belief that eating animal parts improves health
6. (a)   7. false
8. Answers may vary.
9. To protect wildlife
10. Import bans placed on them
11. very profitable/very old tradition
12. Answers may vary.

PAGE 29 - *Activities*

Word Study
1. entire   2. almost
3. proposed   4. nations
5. less   6. roaming
7. bans   8. diseases
9. cruel   10. opportunity

Language
1. expensive   2. wild   3. dense
4. illegal   5. ancient

Answers may vary, teacher check

PAGE 30 The Automobile - *Cloze*

1. driven   2. developed
3. gain   4. explodes
5. recharged   6. passed
7. warn   8. built
9. stood   10. added
11. replaced   12. made
13. shatter   14. breathe
15. kill

PAGE 31 - *Comprehension*

1. It did not shatter into dangerous splinters.
2. to warn pedestrians
3. Germany
4. Answers may vary.
5. (a) 3 (b) 5 (c) 4 (d) 1 (e) 2
6. false
7. batteries had to be recharged
8. (b)
9. hand built by craftsmen
10. pollution and road deaths
11. pneumatic
12. Answers may vary.

PAGE 32 - *Activities*

Language
1. hated   2. using   3. travel
4. exposed   5. damaged

Exposition
1. Answers may vary.

Activity
Teacher check.

PAGE 33 The First Fleet - *Cloze*

1. first   2. miserable
3. leaky   4. terrible
5. damp   6. welcome
7. fresh   8. violent
9. suitable   10. scarce
11. new   12. dangerous
13. magnificent   14. deep
15. east

PAGE 34 - *Comprehension*

1. Scurvy killed many sailors
2. green vegetables
3. south 1.4 (c)
4. to carry convicts
5. scarce water, poor soil, too strong (winds)
6. false   7. (c)
8. eight months
9. Answers may vary.
10. leaky
11. (a) fact (b) opinion (c) opinion

PAGE 35 - *Activities*

Language
1. difficult   2. cruel   3. return
4. domesticated 5. last

Brainstorming
Answers may vary. Teacher check.

Report
Answers may vary. Teacher check.

PAGE 36 Spring - *Cloze*

1. time   2. green   3. gather
4. where   5. shorter   6. players
7. hot   8. colorful 9. broken
10. washing 11. dawns
12. happy   13. smooth
14. lambs   15. butterflies

PAGE 37 - *Comprehension*

1. false
2. Answers may vary. (sail, move, swim)
3. calm seas   4. bleating
5. lawn-mowers
6. they are swinging bats
7. flowers   8. (c)
9. trees with no leaves
10. lea
11. both are flying from flower to flower
12. Answers may vary.

PAGE 38 - *Activities*

Word Study
1. glowing   2. frolic   3. quiet
4. gone   5. build   6. glide
7. see   8. time   9. show
10. happy

Report
Answers may vary. Teacher check.

Poetic Text
Answers may vary. Teacher check.

PAGE 39 Florence Nightingale-*Cloze*

1. childhood 2. days   3. group
4. Britain   5. hospital
6. conditions 7. patients
8. lamp   9. officers 10. medals
11. money   12. School 13. illness
14. woman   15. life

PAGE 40 - *Comprehension*

1. France   2. rats
3. false   4. Answers may vary.
5. 34
6. she was born in Florence
7. Order of Merit 8. character traits

Trait	Not	Fairly	Very	Can't Tell	Reason for Answer
Caring			✔		
Selfish	✔				
Modest			✔		
Generous			✔		
Comical				✔	

9. 90
10. Answers may vary, e.g. cleaned up and got rid of rats
11. fewer soldiers died 12. (c)

PAGE 41 - *Activities*

Word Study
1. refused   2. horrified
3. gradually   4. filthy
5. wealthy   6. childhood
7. few   8. found
9. war   10. sick

Language
1. pioneer   2. hospitals
3. nursing   4. war time
5. nurses

Narrative
Answers may vary. Teacher check.

PAGE 42 Oliver Twist - *Cloze*

1. wrote   2. dies   3. began
4. requested 5. punished 6. met
7. introduced 8. organized 9. forced
10. heard   11. hanged
12. sentenced 13. imprisoned
14. adopted   15. led

PAGE 43 - *Comprehension*

1. London   2. Jack Dawkins
3. Mr. Brownlow
4. insolence. Answers may vary.
5. because he worked hard
6. true
7. he was badly treated
8. No. Answers may vary.
9. forced
10. to make him a member of the gang
11. (c) 12. Answers may vary.

PAGE 44 - *Activities*

Word Study
1. imprisoned   2. novelist
3. cruel   4. impudence
5. pickpockets 6. artful
7. forced   8. lived
9. wretched   10. areas

	Dickens	Oliver's mother	Fagin	Oliver	Sykes	Mr Brownlow	Jack
Kind	✔					✔	
Rich	✔					✔	
Poor		✔		✔			
Cruel			✔		✔		
Hardworking	✔			✔			
Criminal			✔		✔		✔

Exposition
Answers may vary. Teacher check.

PAGE 45 Deserts - *Cloze*

1. hot or cold   2. for their animals
3. for centuries   4. for years
5. at night   6. by flies
7. in the oases   8. on the edges
9. Because of over grazing
10. of trees   11. In richer countries

12. over long distances
13. in some desert populations
14. like cotton   15. in poverty

PAGE 46 - *Comprehension*

1. dust storms   2. goats
3. trachoma   4. (b)
5. too many animals grazing on land
6. fertilizers, animal manure
7. nomads   8. (c)
9. Answers may vary.
10. the skies are so clear
11. in richer countries
12. (a) fact (b) fact (c) opinion
    (d) opinion

PAGE 47 - *Activities*

Report
   Answers may vary. Teacher check.
Ordering Preferences
   Answers may vary. Teacher check.
Map Exercise
   Teacher check.

PAGE 48 Earthquakes - *Cloze*

1. layers   2. floats   3. liquid
4. Earth   5. broken
6. Earthquakes 7. collide
8. smaller   9. giant
10. drown   11. epicenter
12. devastated 13. estimated
14. sway   15. construction

PAGE 49 - *Comprehension*

1. mantle   2. true
3. tsunamis
4. answers may vary, violent
5. China
6. (a) 4 (b) 3 (c) 1 (d) 2
7. earthquakes under the sea
8. intense heat
9. they float on the mantle
10. fault lines
11. aftershocks
12(a) fact (b) opinion (c) fact (d) fact

PAGE 50 - *Activities*

Word Study
   1. strong   2. edges
   3. occur   4. devastated
   5. liquid   6. collide
   7. intense   8. giant
   9. died   10. sway
Character Self-Portrait
   Answers may vary. Teacher check.

Books Available from World Teachers Press®

MATH

A Blast of Math
Grades 3-4, 4-5, 5-6, 6-7

Math Word Puzzles
Grades 5-8

Mastergrids for Math
Elementary Resource

Essential Facts and Tables
Grades 3-10

Math Puzzles Galore
Grades 4-8

Practice Math
Grades 4, 5, 6, 7

Math Speed Tests
Grades 1-3, 3-6

Problem Solving with Math
Grades 2-3, 4-5, 6-8

Math Through Language
Grades 1-2, 2-3, 3-4

Exploring Measurement
Grades 2-3, 3-4, 5-6

Chance, Statistics & Graphs
Grades 1-3, 3-5

Step Into Tables
Elementary

Problem Solving Through Investigation
Grades 5-8, 7-10

The Early Fraction Book
Grades 3-4

The Fraction Book
Grades 5-8

It's About Time
Grades 2-3, 4-5

Do It Write Math
Grades 2-3

Mental Math Workouts
Grades 4-6, 5-7, 6-8, 7-9

Math Grid Games
Grades 4-8

High Interest Mathematics
Grades 5-8

Math Homework Assignments
Grades 2, 3, 4, 5, 6, 7

Visual Discrimination
Grades 1-12

Active Math

Math Enrichment
Grades 4-7

Time Tables Challenge

30 Math Games
PreK-1

Early Skills Series:
Addition to Five, Counting and Recognition to Five, Cutting Activities, Early Visual Skills

Spatial Relations
Grades 1-2, 3-4, 5-6

High Interest Geometry
Grades 5-8

Money Matters
Grades 1, 2, 3

LANGUAGE ARTS

Multiple-Choice Comprehension
Grades 2-3, 4-5, 6-7

My Desktop Dictionary
Grades 2-5

Spelling Essentials
Grades 3-10

Reading for Detail
Grades 4-5, 6-7

Writing Frameworks
Grades 2-3, 4-5, 6-7

Spelling Success
Grades 1, 2, 3, 4, 5, 6, 7

My Junior Spelling Journal
Grades 1-2

My Spelling Journal
Grades 3-6

Cloze Encounters
Grades 1-2, 3-4, 5-6

Comprehension Lifters
1, 2, 3, 4

Grammar Skills
Grades 2-3, 4-5, 6-8

Vocabulary Development through Dictionary Skills
Grades 3-4, 5-6, 7-8

Recipes for Readers
Grades 3-6

Step Up To Comprehension
Grades 2-3, 4-5, 6-8

Cloze
Grades 2-3, 4-5, 6-8

Cloze in on Language
Grades 3-5, 4-6, 5-7, 6-8

Initial Sounds Fold-Ups

Phonic Sound Cards

Early Activity Phonics

Activity Phonics

Early Phonics in Context

Phonics in Context

Build-A-Reader

Communicating
Grades 5-6

Oral Language
Grades 2-3, 4-5, 6-8

Listen! Hear!
Grades 1-2, 3-4, 5-6

Phonic Fold-Ups

Word Study
Grades 2-3, 4-5, 6-7, 7-8

Draw to a Cloze
Grades 5-8

Classical Literature
Grades 3-4, 5-6, 5-8

High Interest Vocabulary
Grades 5-8

Literacy Lifters
1, 2, 3, 4

Look! Listen! Think!
Grades 2-3, 4-5, 6-7

Teach Editing
Grades 2-3, 3-4, 5-6

Proofreading and Editing
Grades 3-4, 4-8, 7-8

High Interest Language
Grades 5-8

Comprehend It!
Grades 1-3, 4-5, 6-8

Comprehension for Young Readers

Language Skill Boosters
Grades 1, 2, 3, 4, 5, 6, 7

Phonic Charts

Vocabulary Sleuths
Grades 5-7, 6-9

Early Theme Series:
Bears, Creepy Crawlies, The Sea

Phonics in Action Series:
Initial Sounds, Final Consonant Sounds, Initial Blends and Digraphs, Phonic Pictures

OTHERS

Exploring Change
Grades 3-4, 5-6, 7-8

Ancient Egypt, Ancient Rome, Ancient Greece
Grades 4-7

Australian Aboriginal Culture
Grades 3-4, 5-6, 7-8

Reading Maps
Grades 2-3, 4-5, 6-8

The Music Book
Grades 4-8

Mapping Skills
Grades 2-3, 3-4, 5-6

Introducing The Internet

Internet Theme Series:
Sea, The Solar System, Endangered Species

Art Media

Visit us at:
www.worldteacherspress.com
for further information and free sample pages.